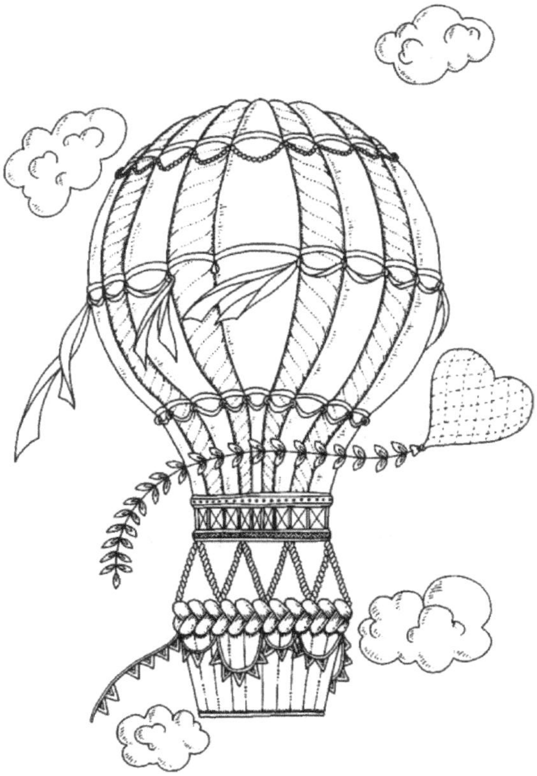

BALLOON PUBLISHING

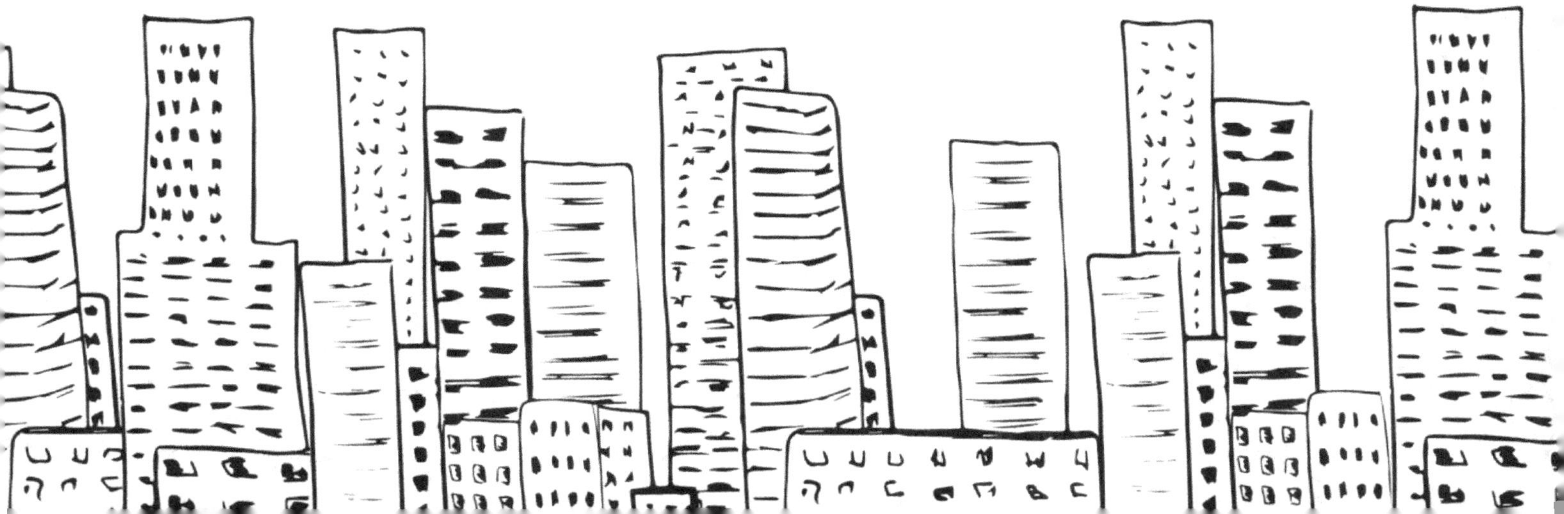

COLOR TEST PAGE

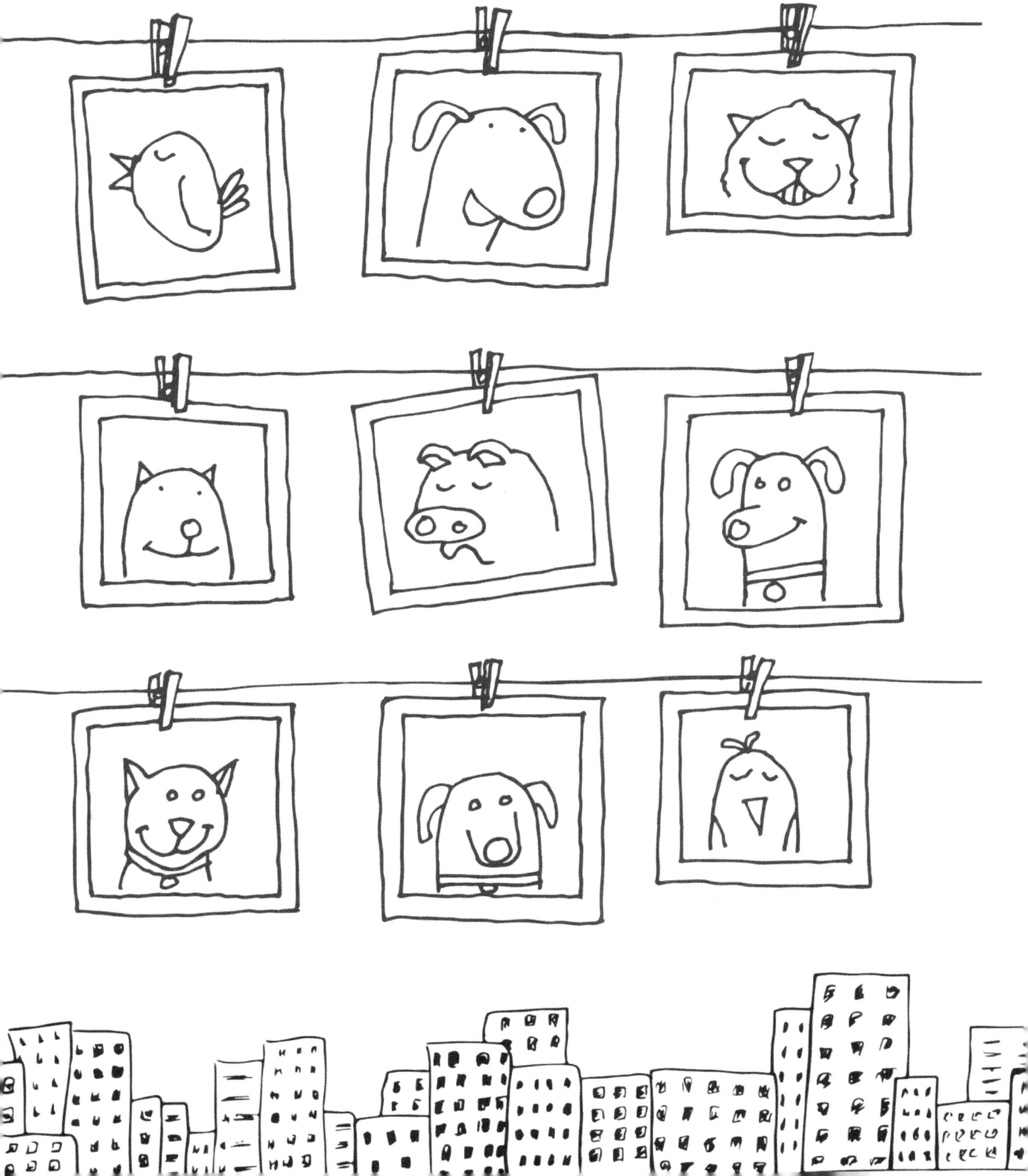

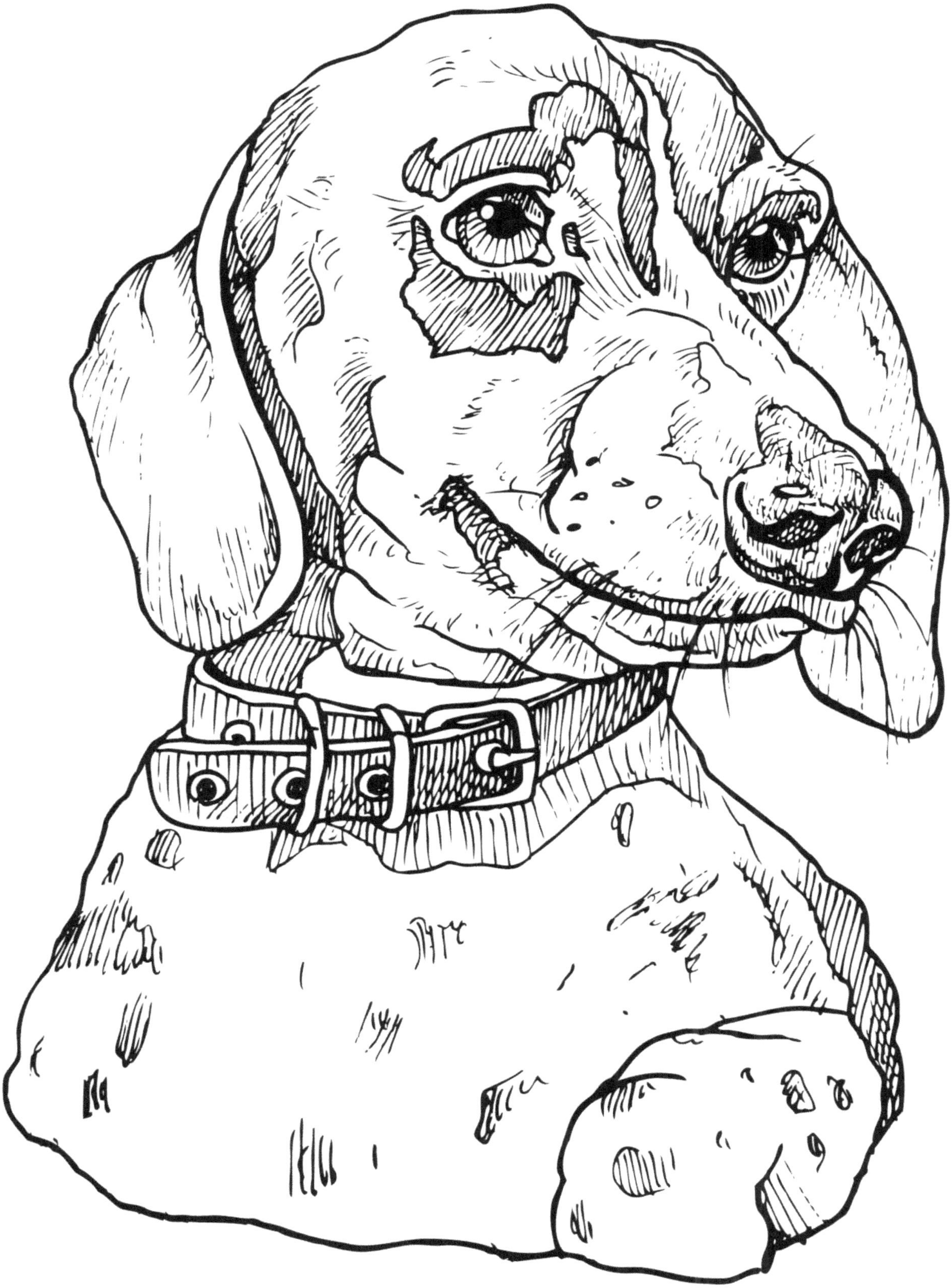

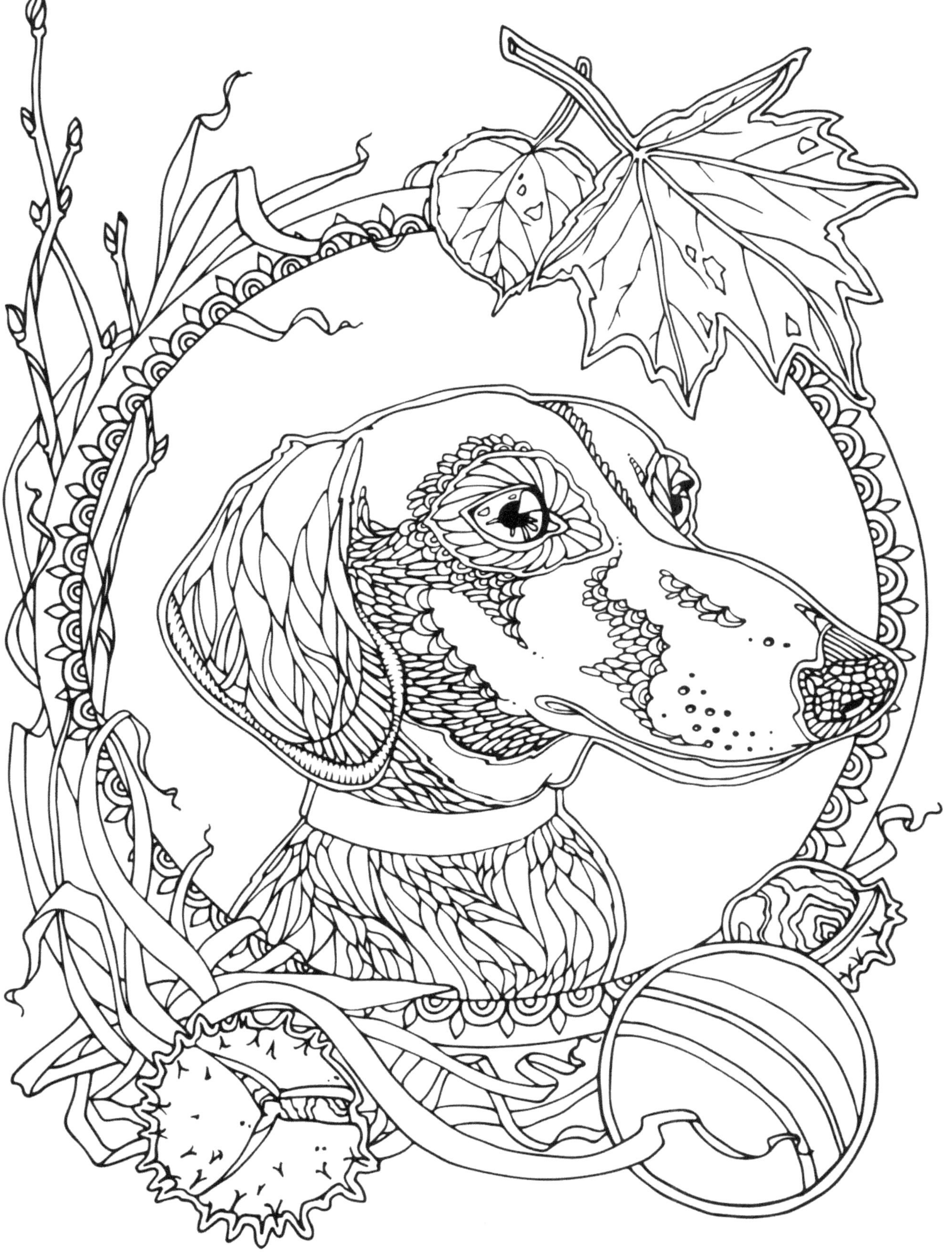

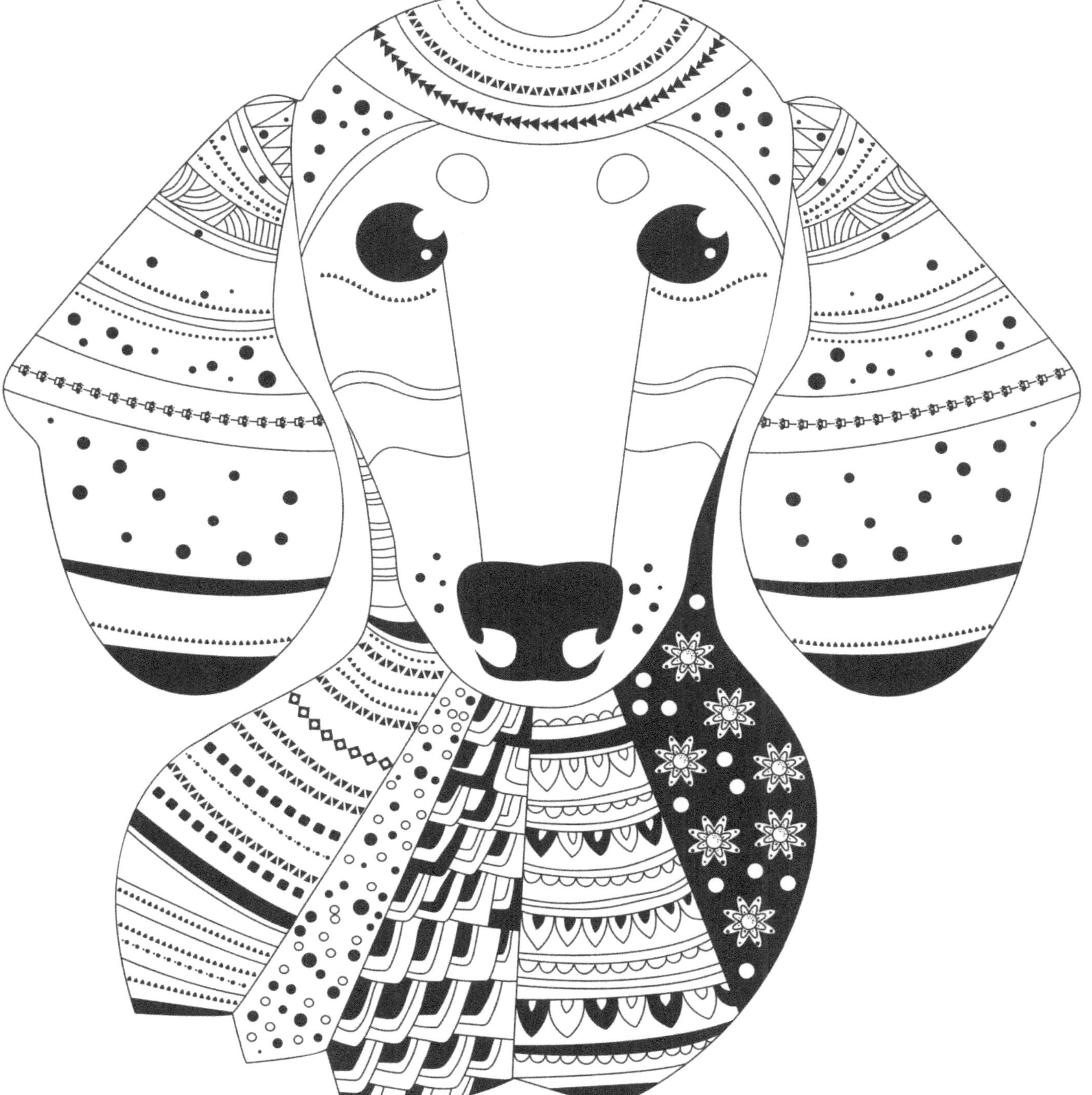

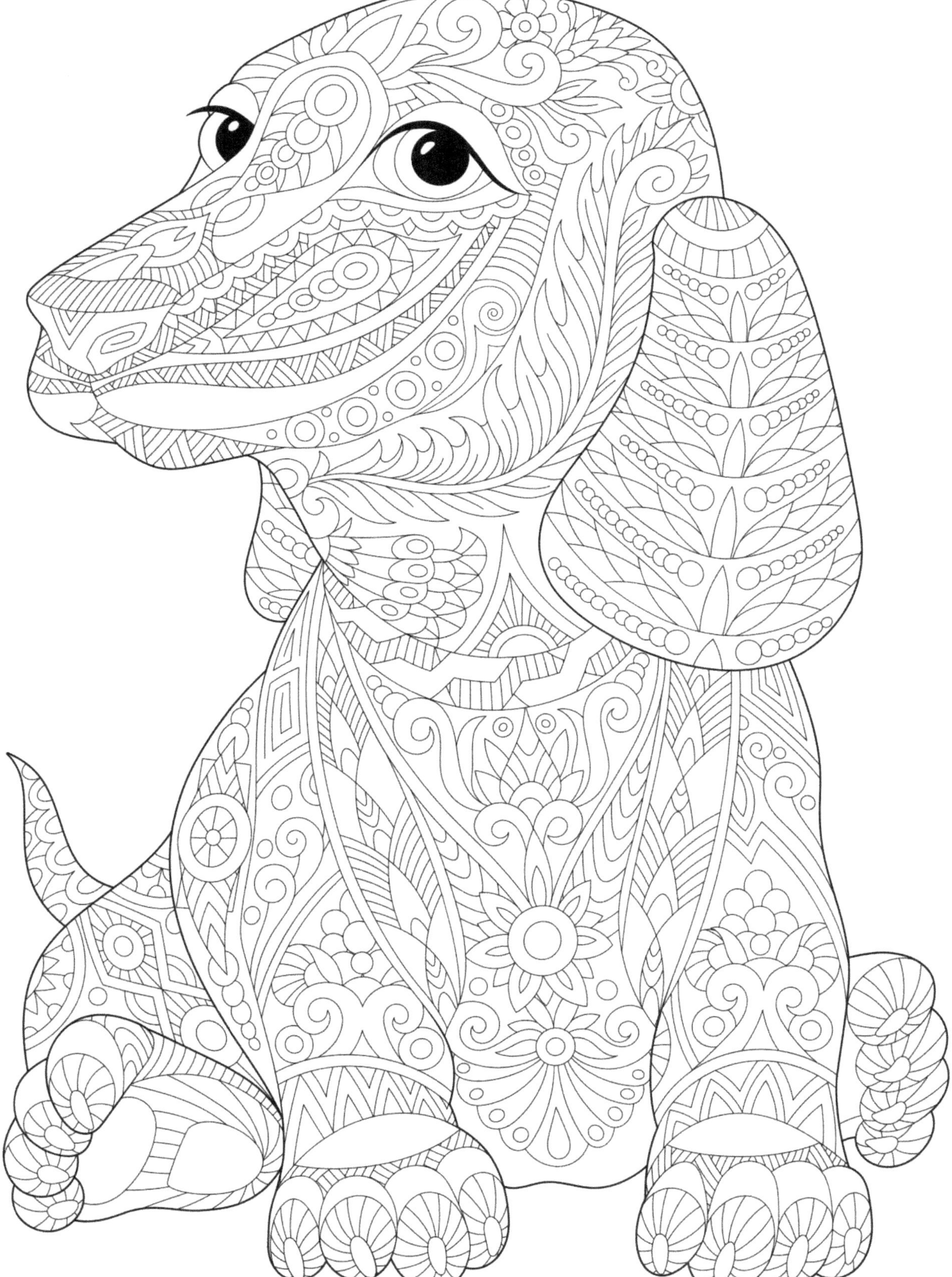

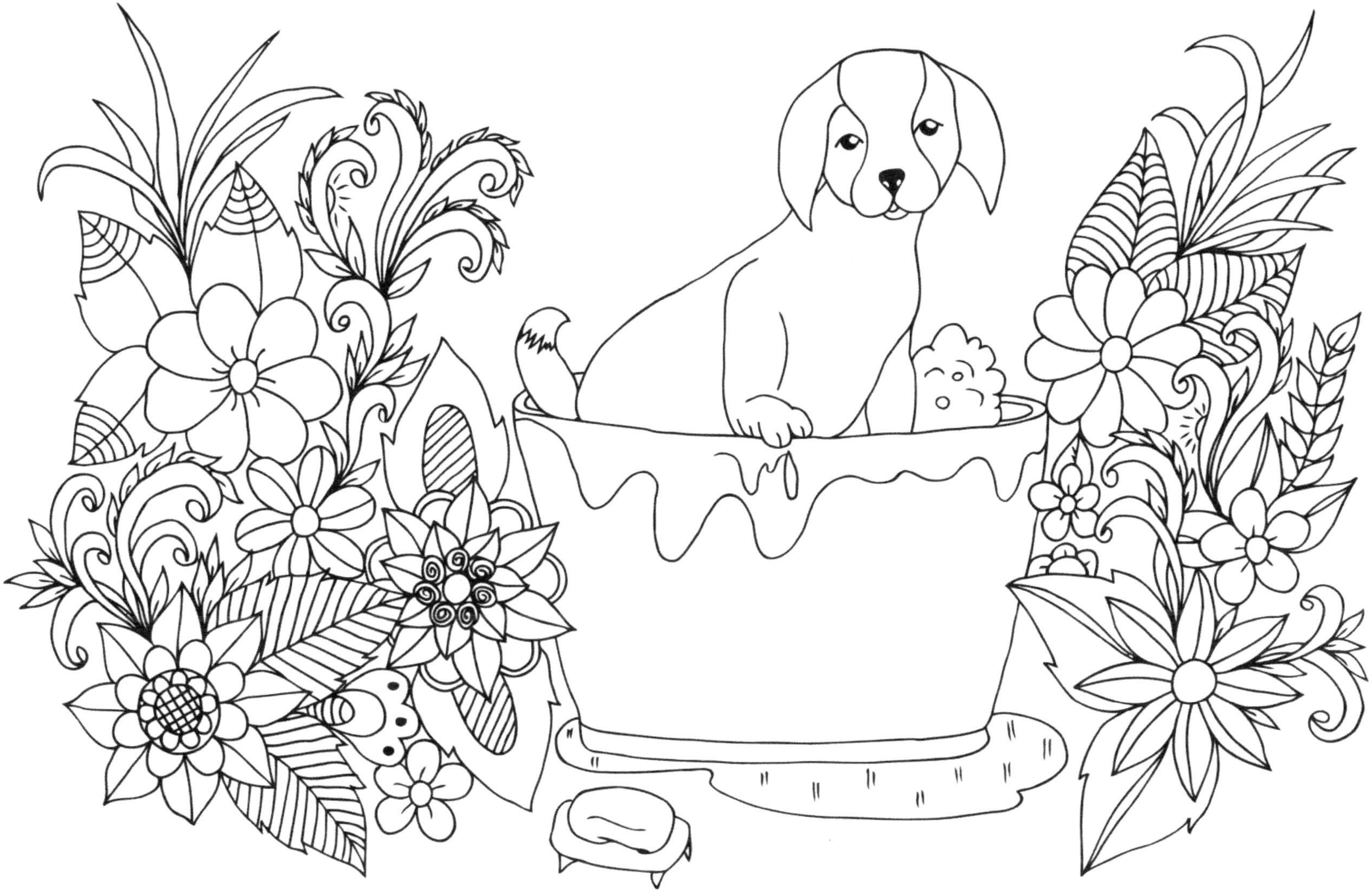

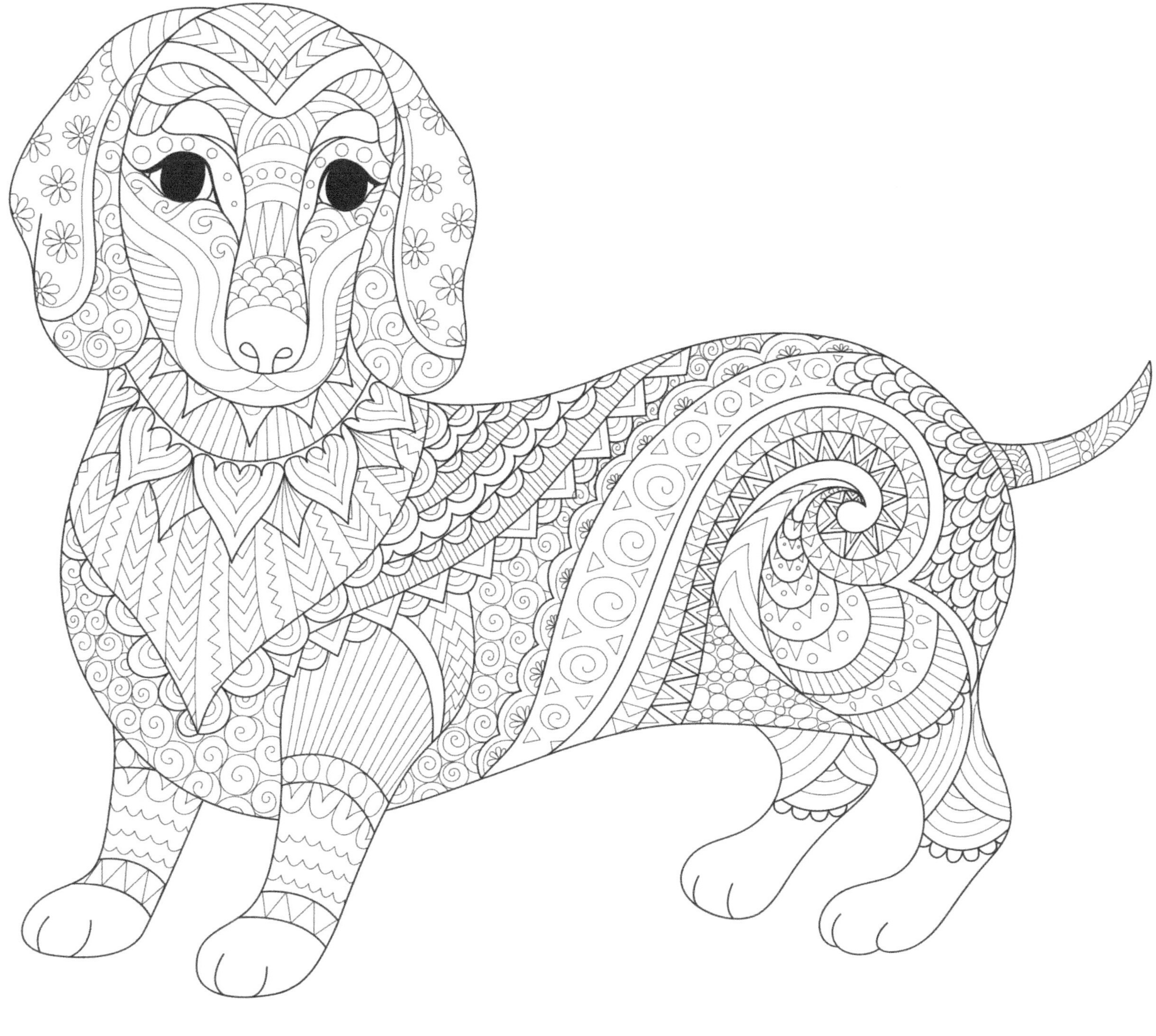

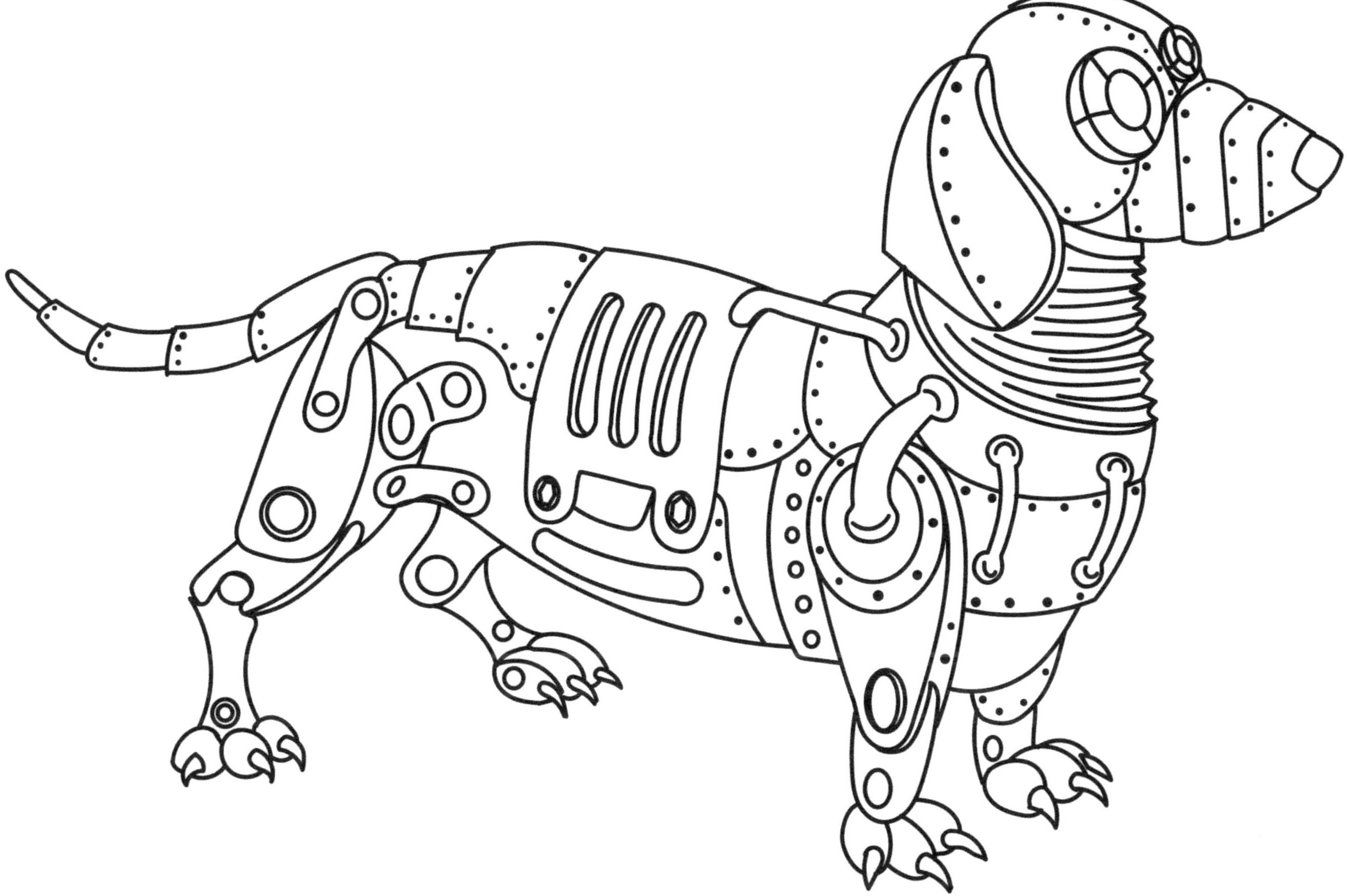

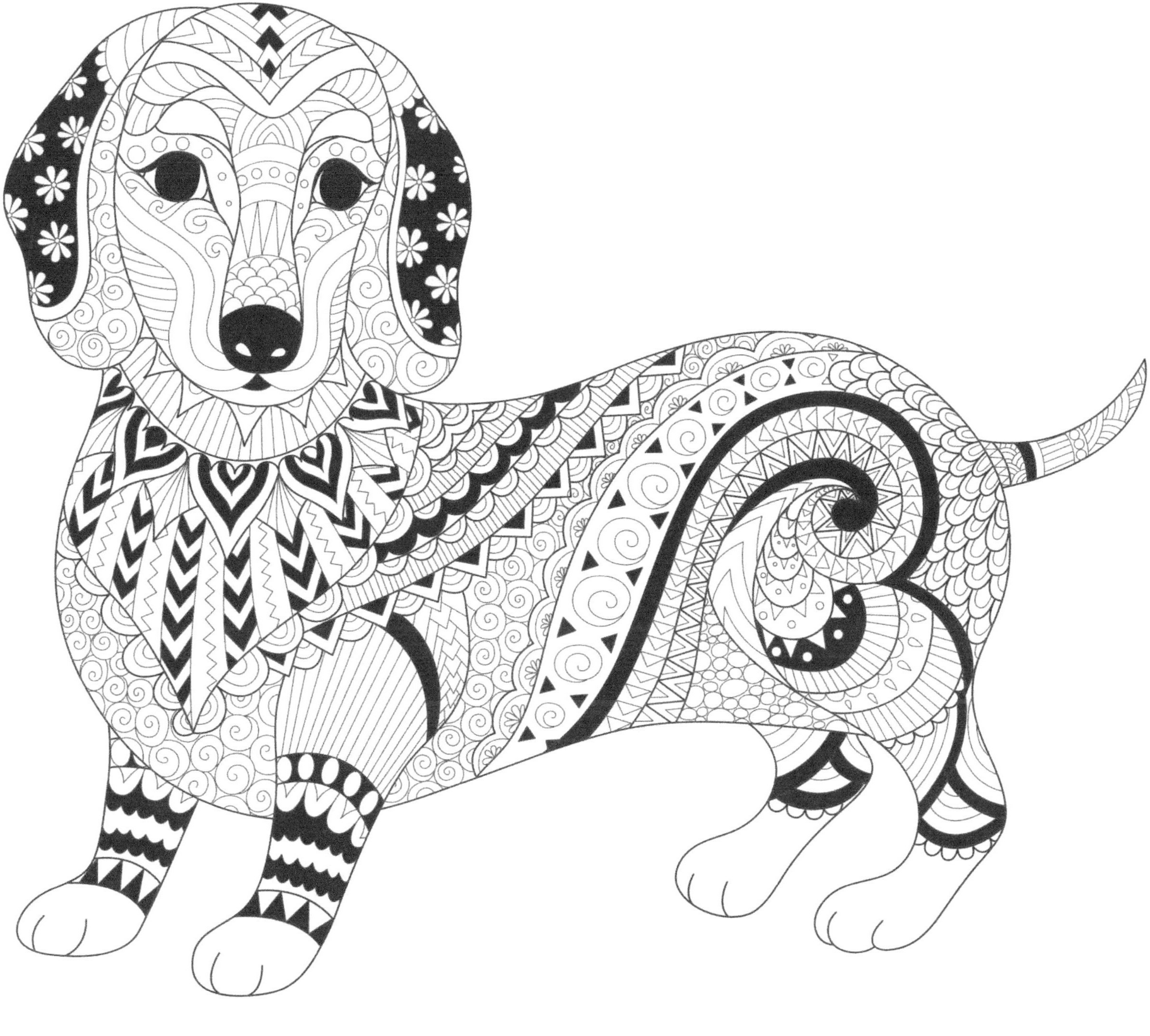

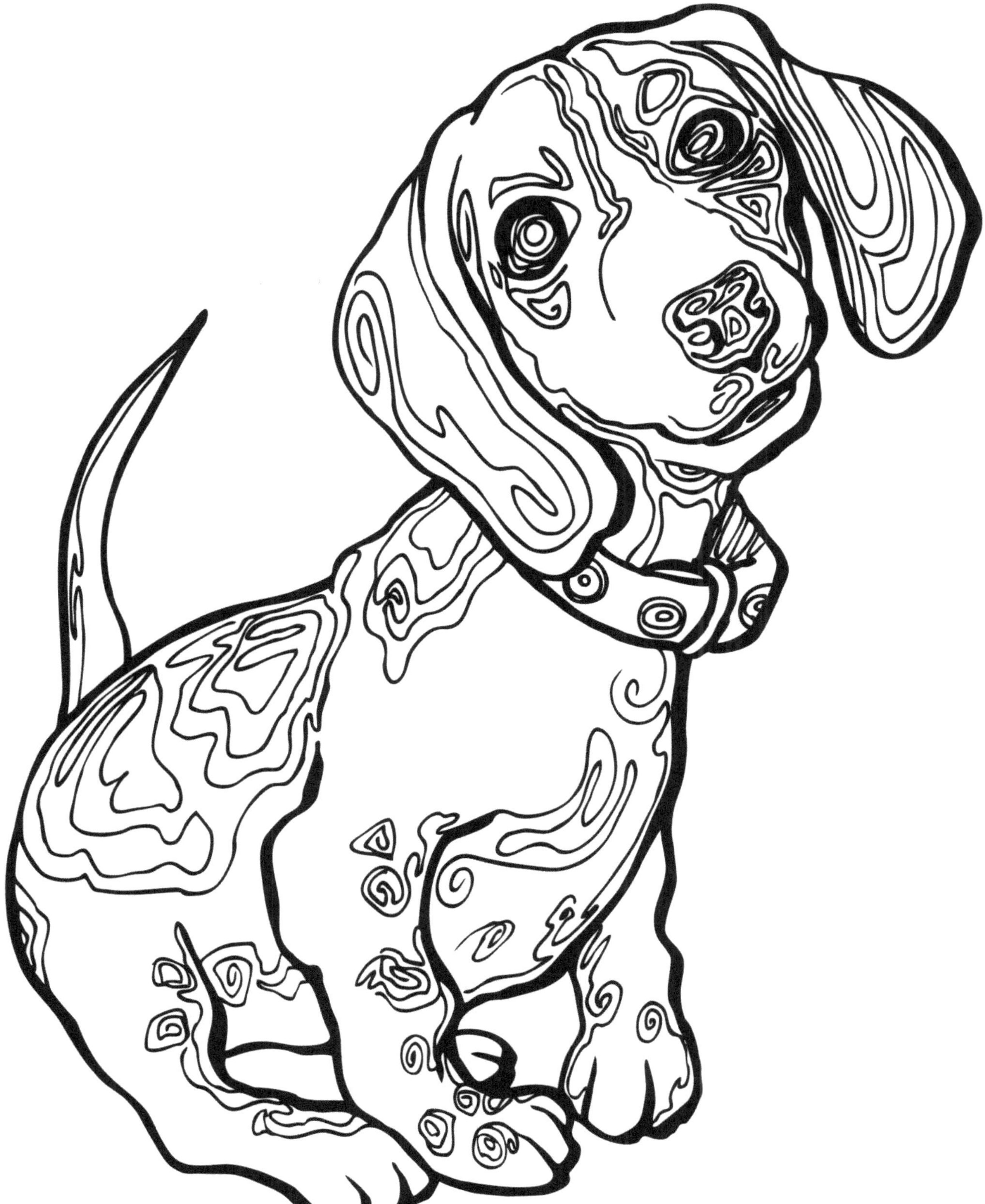

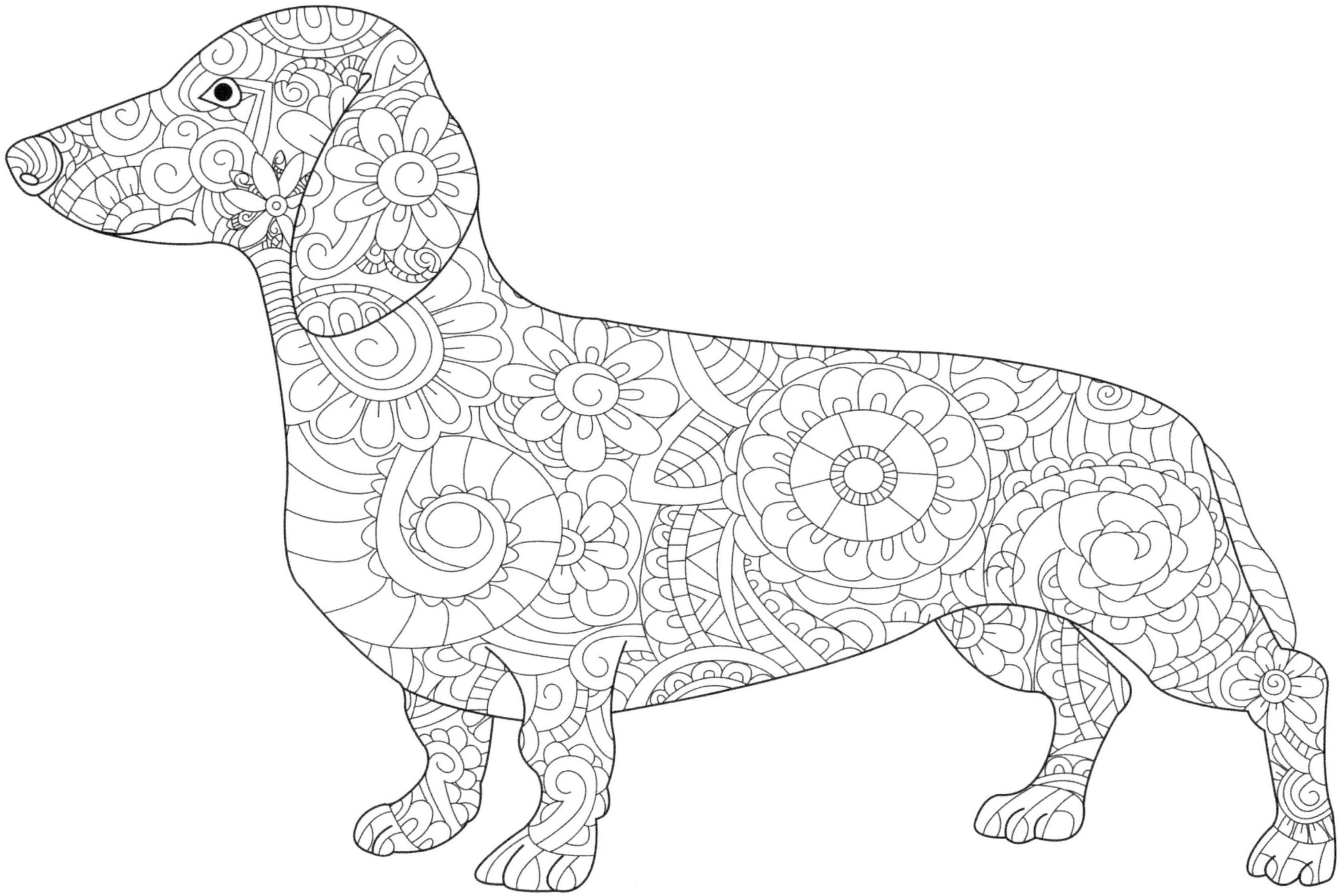

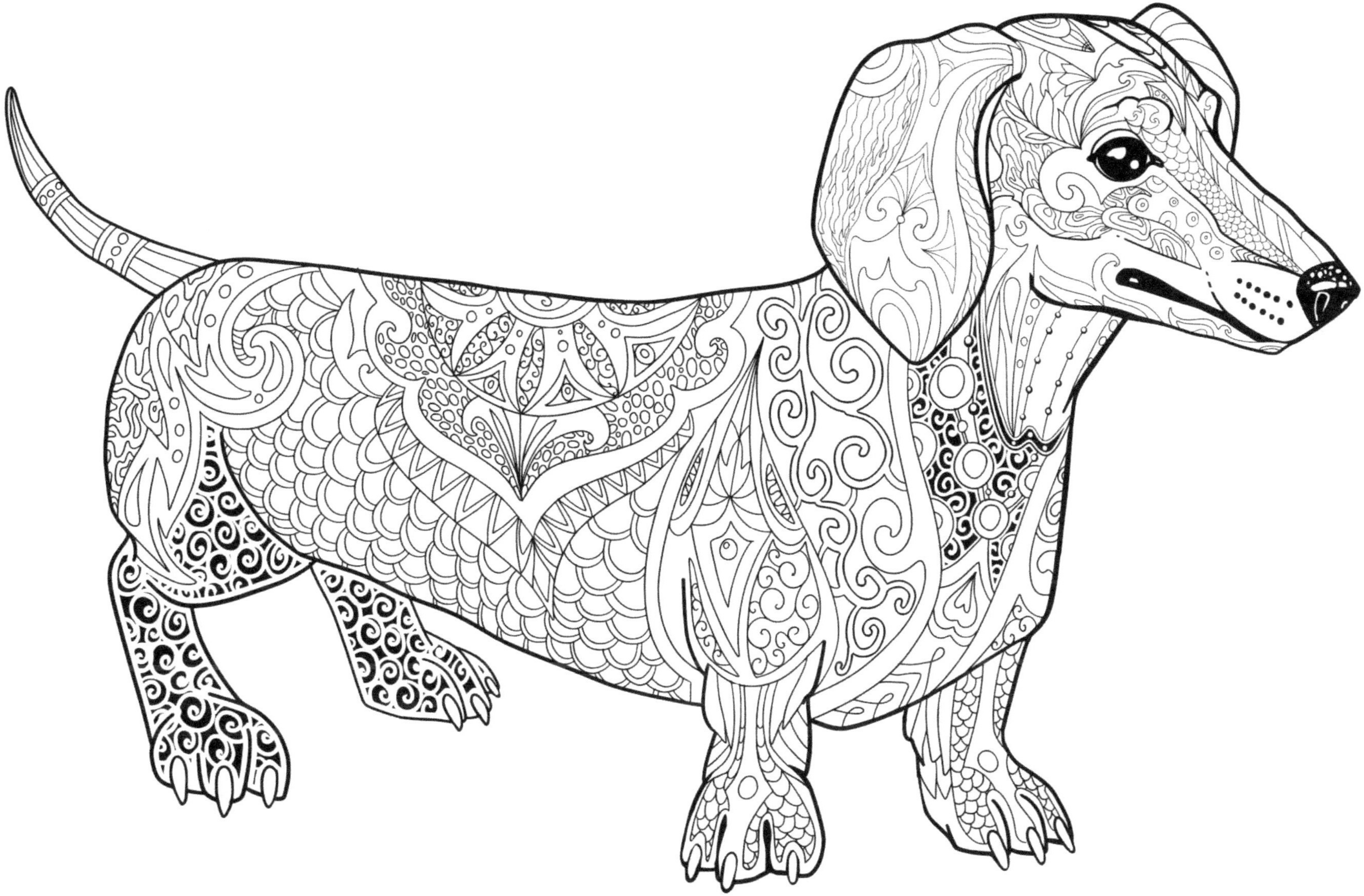

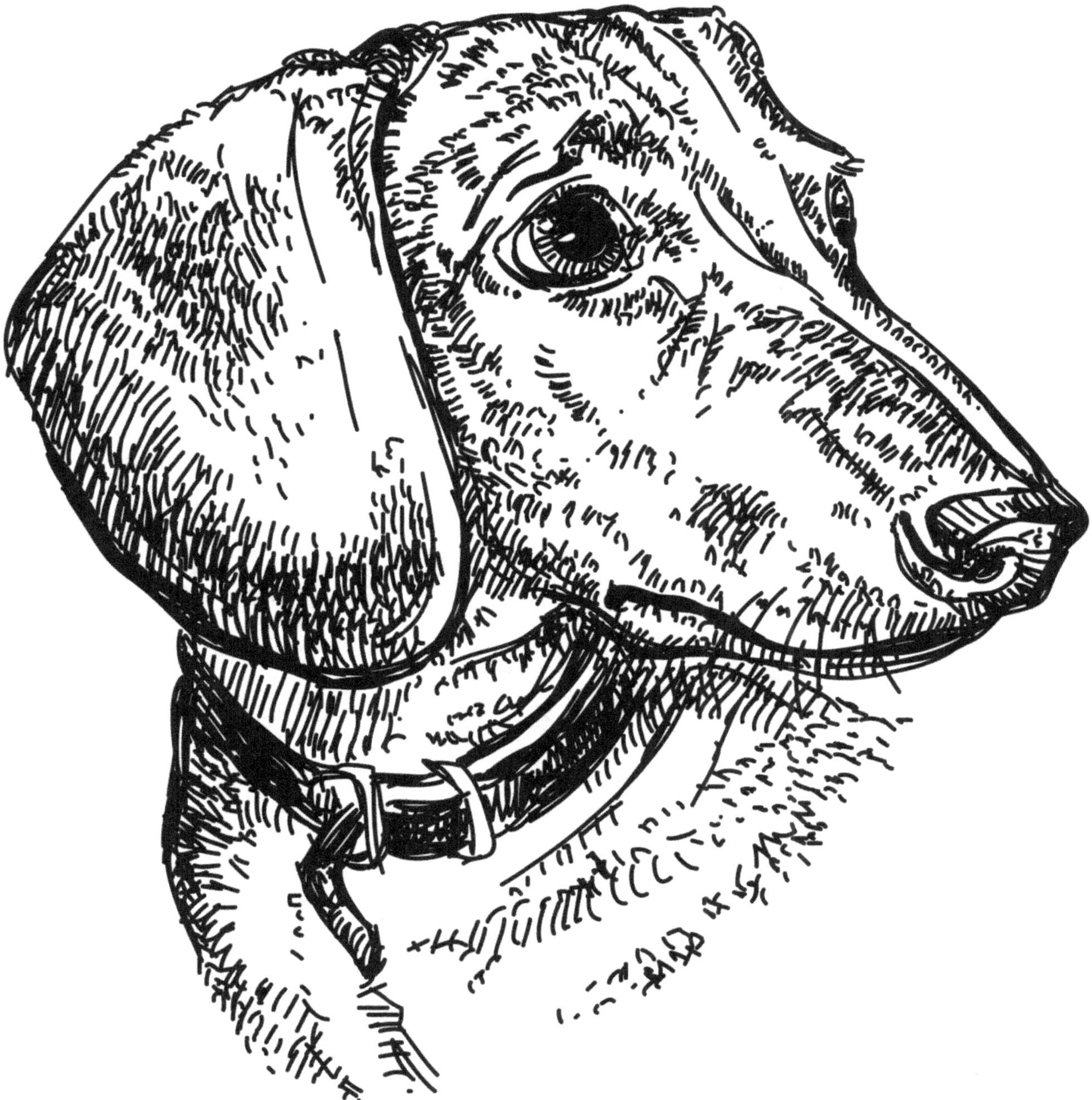

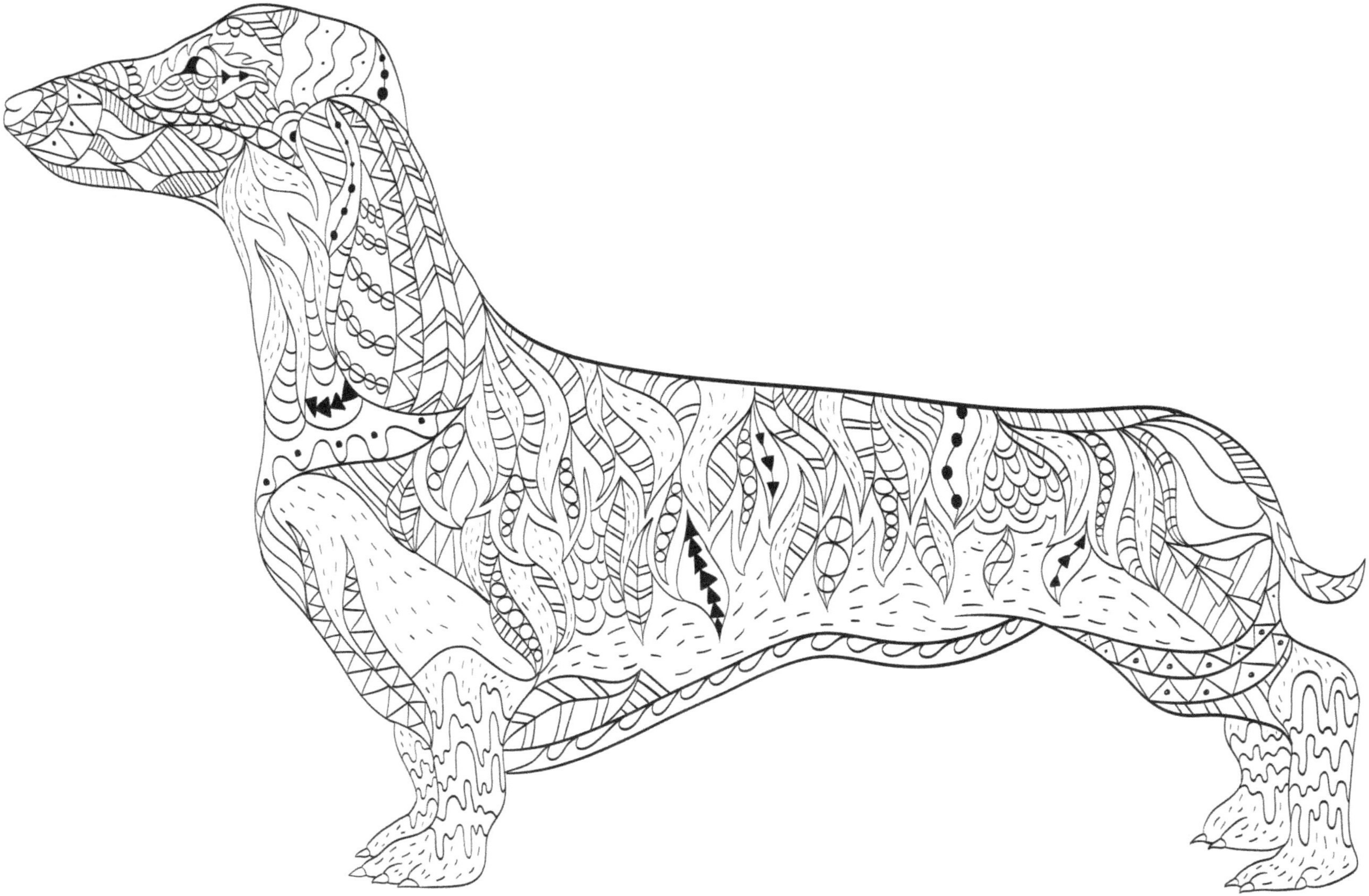

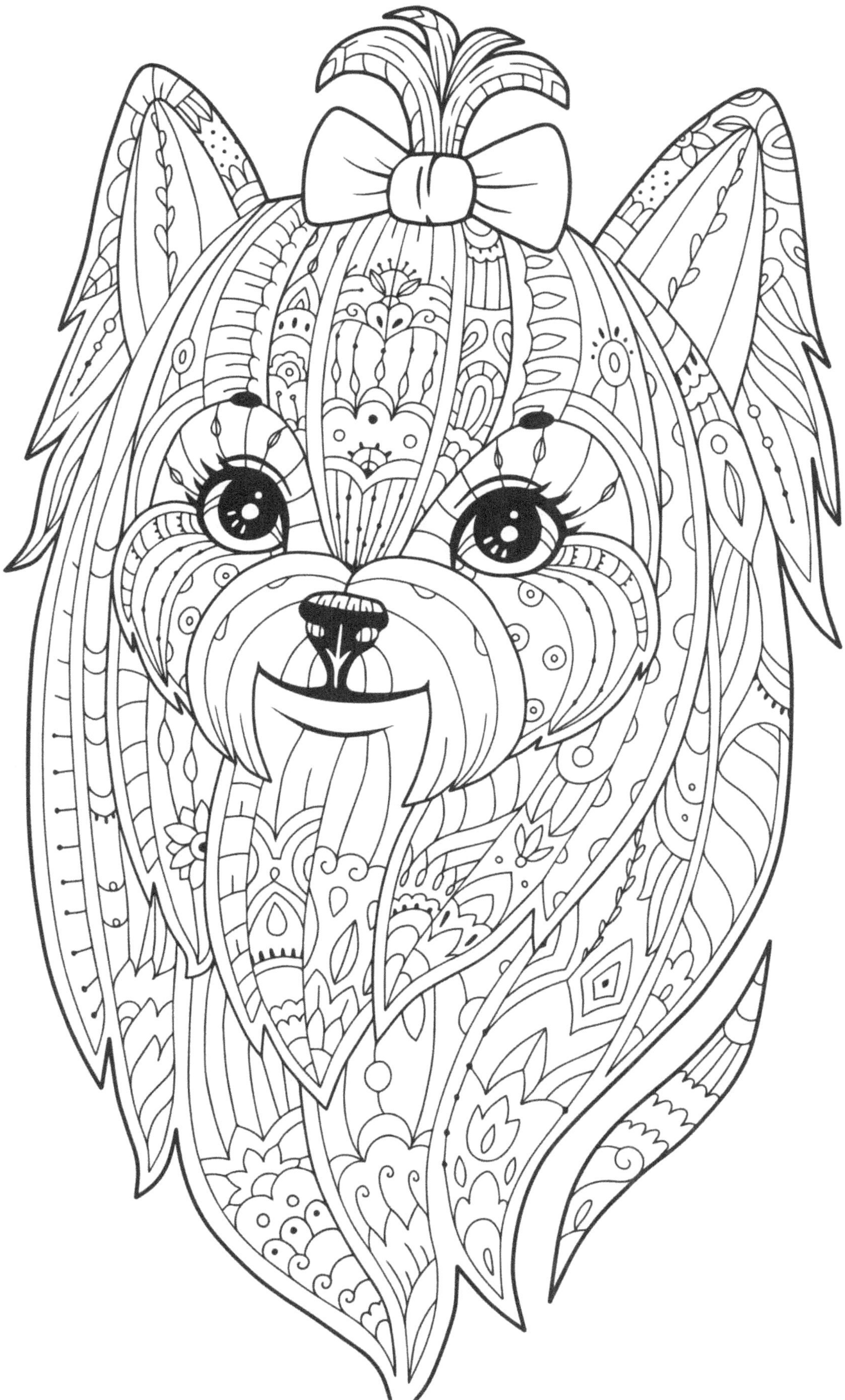

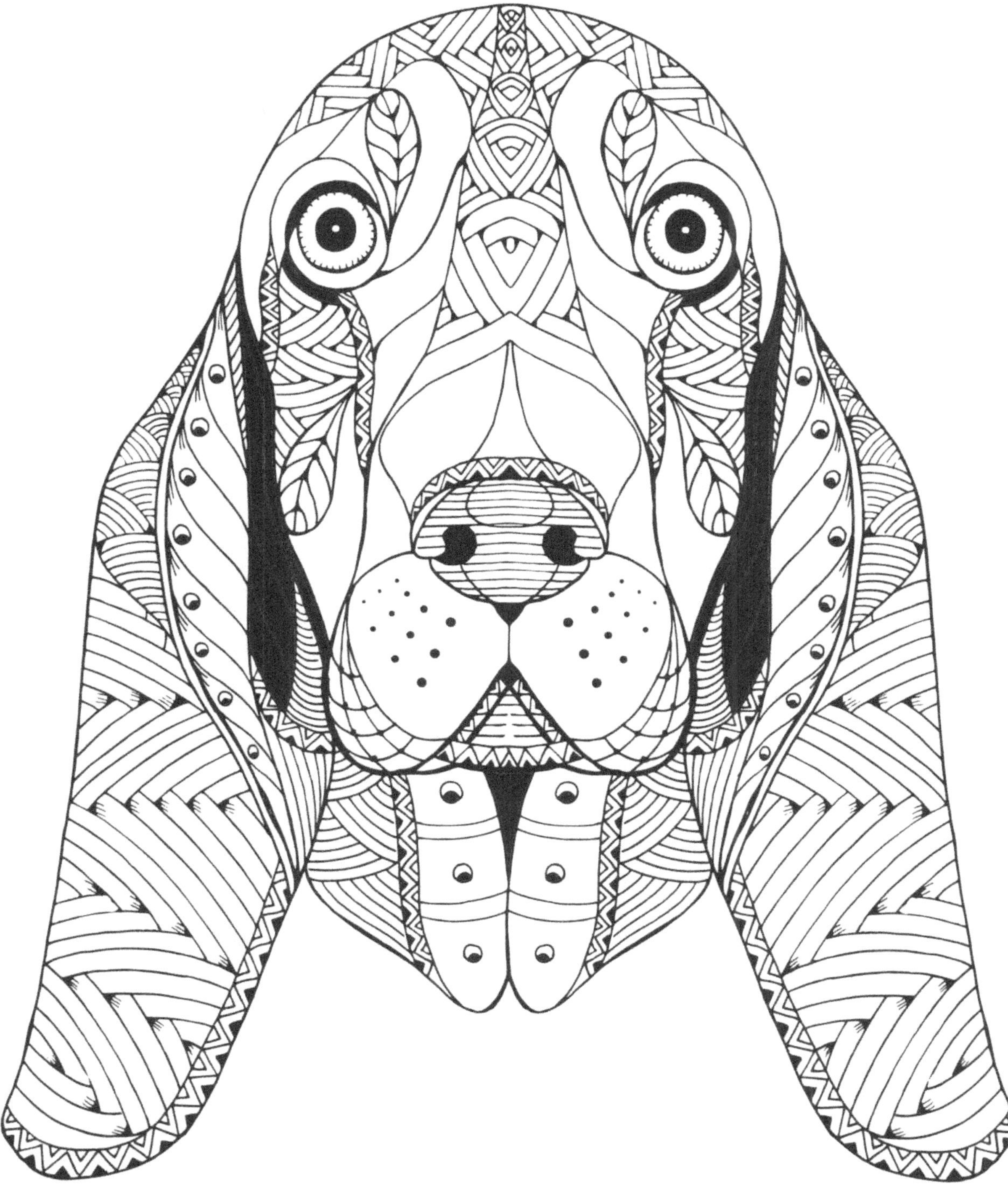

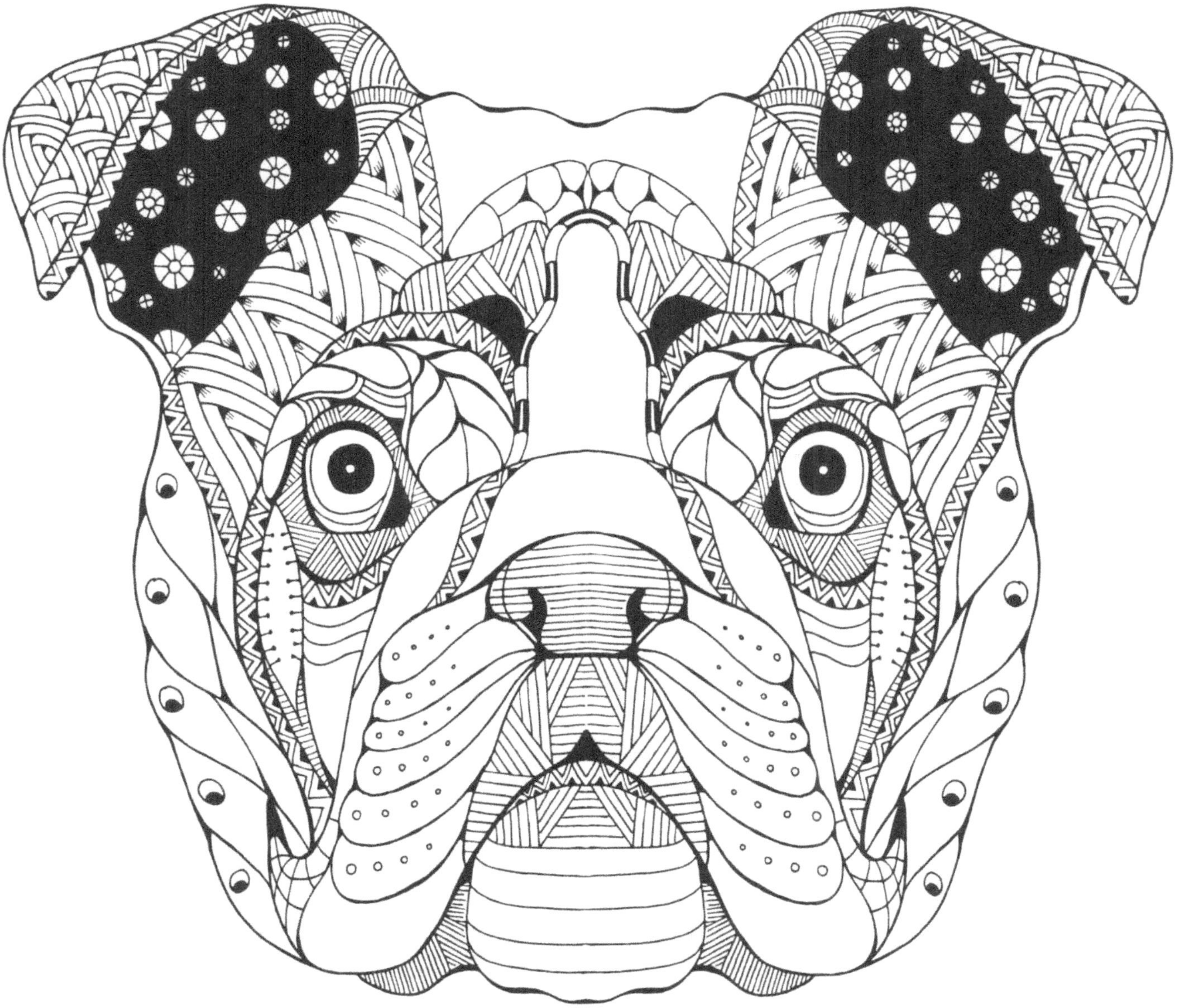

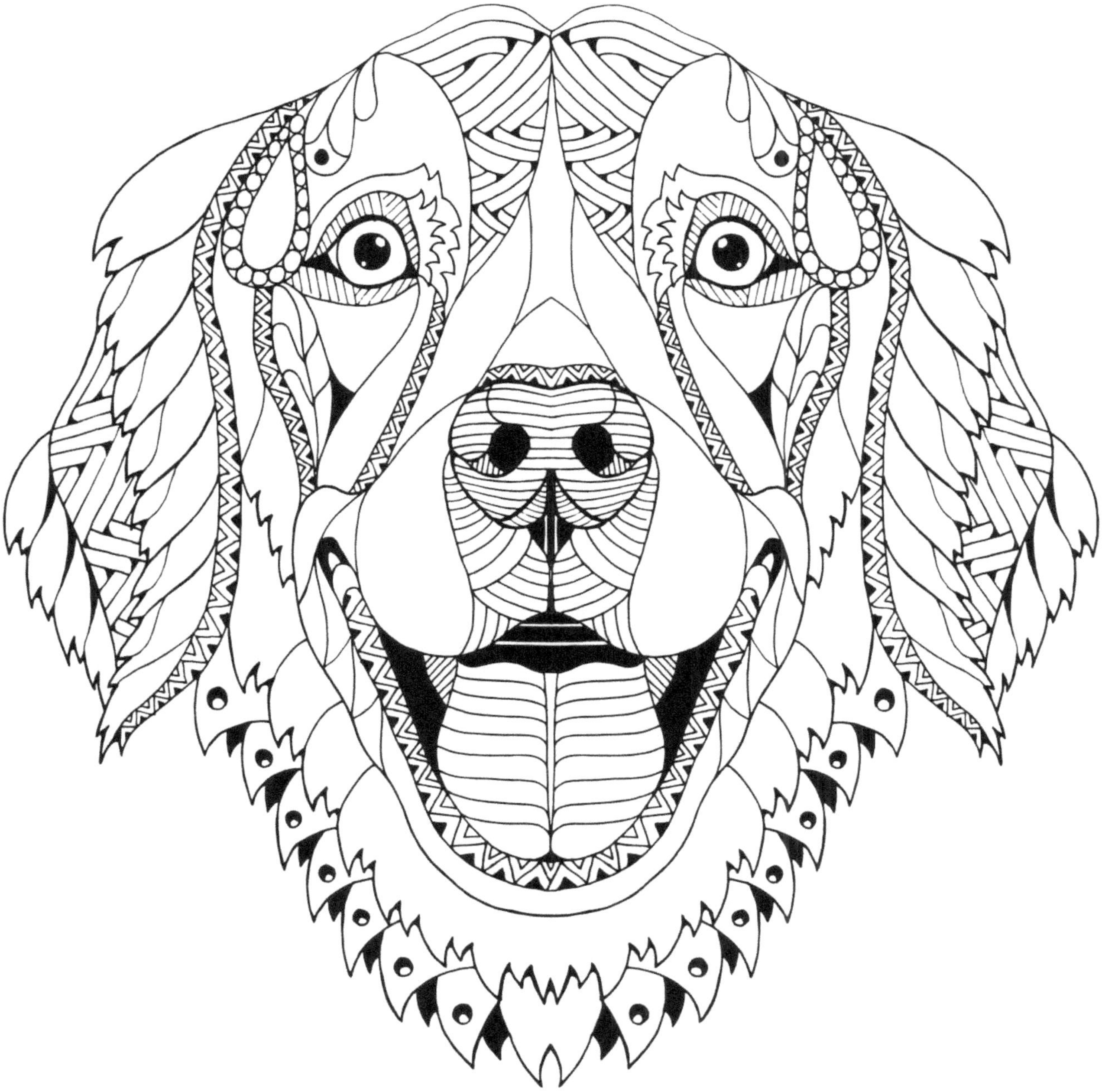

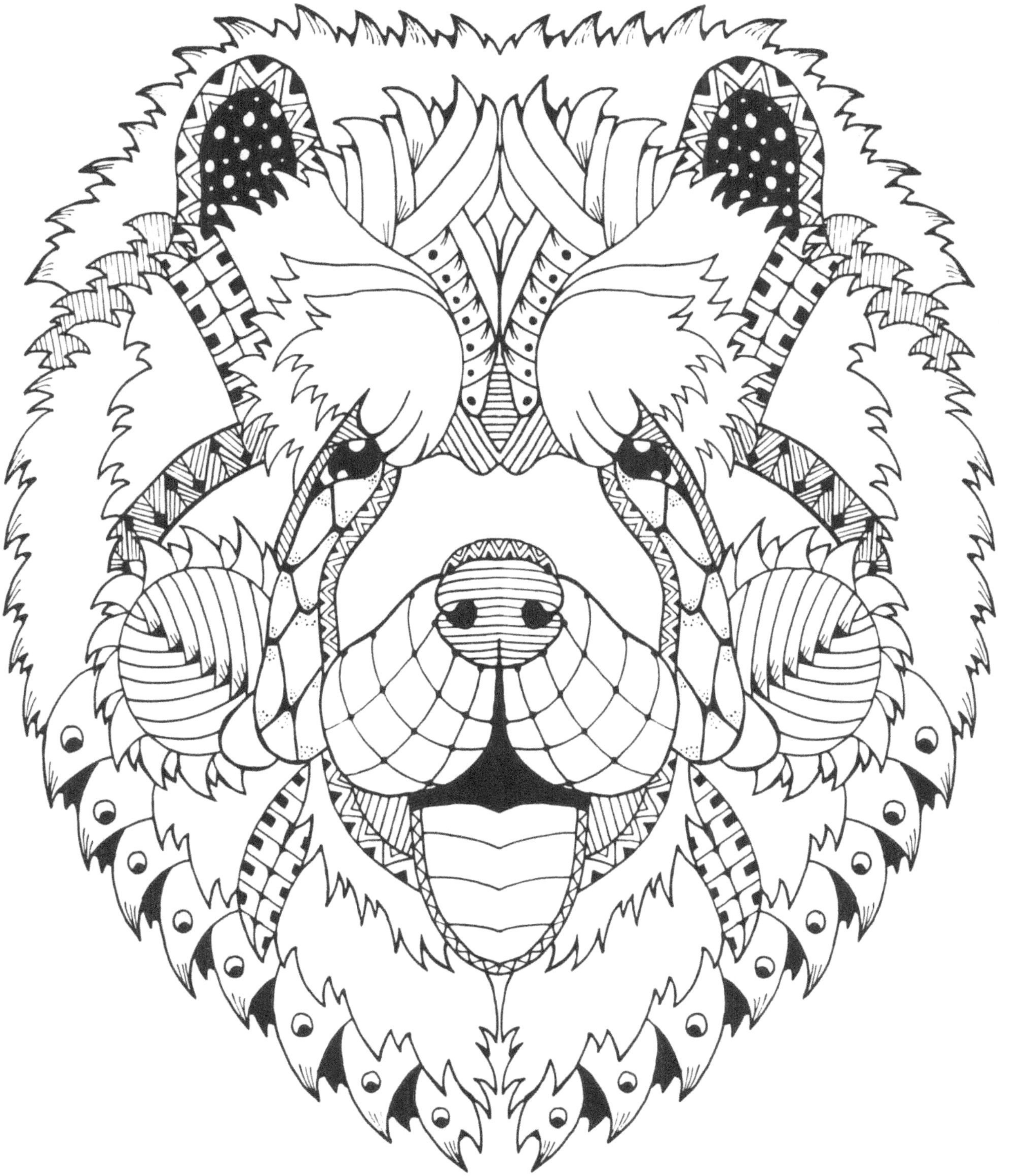

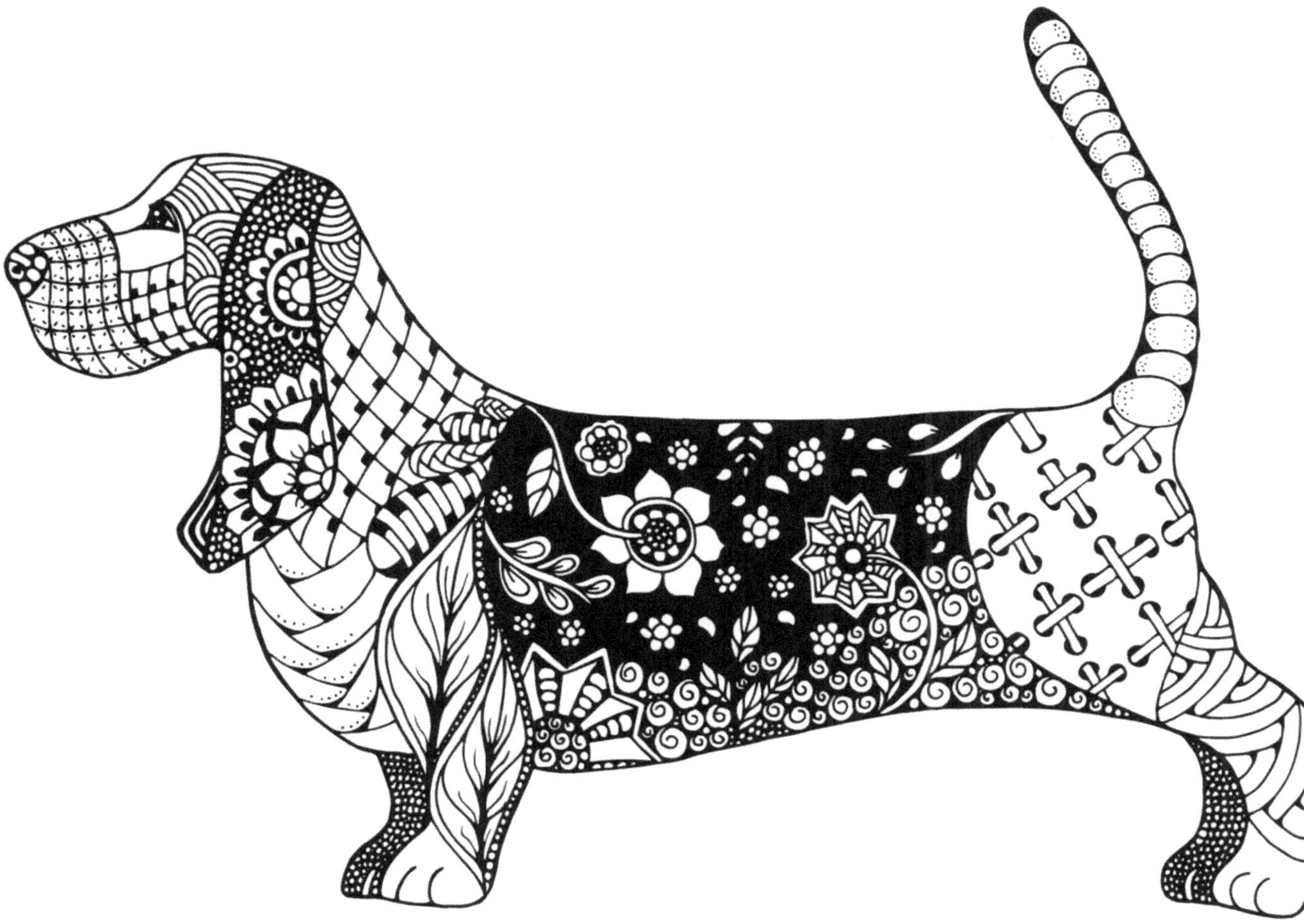

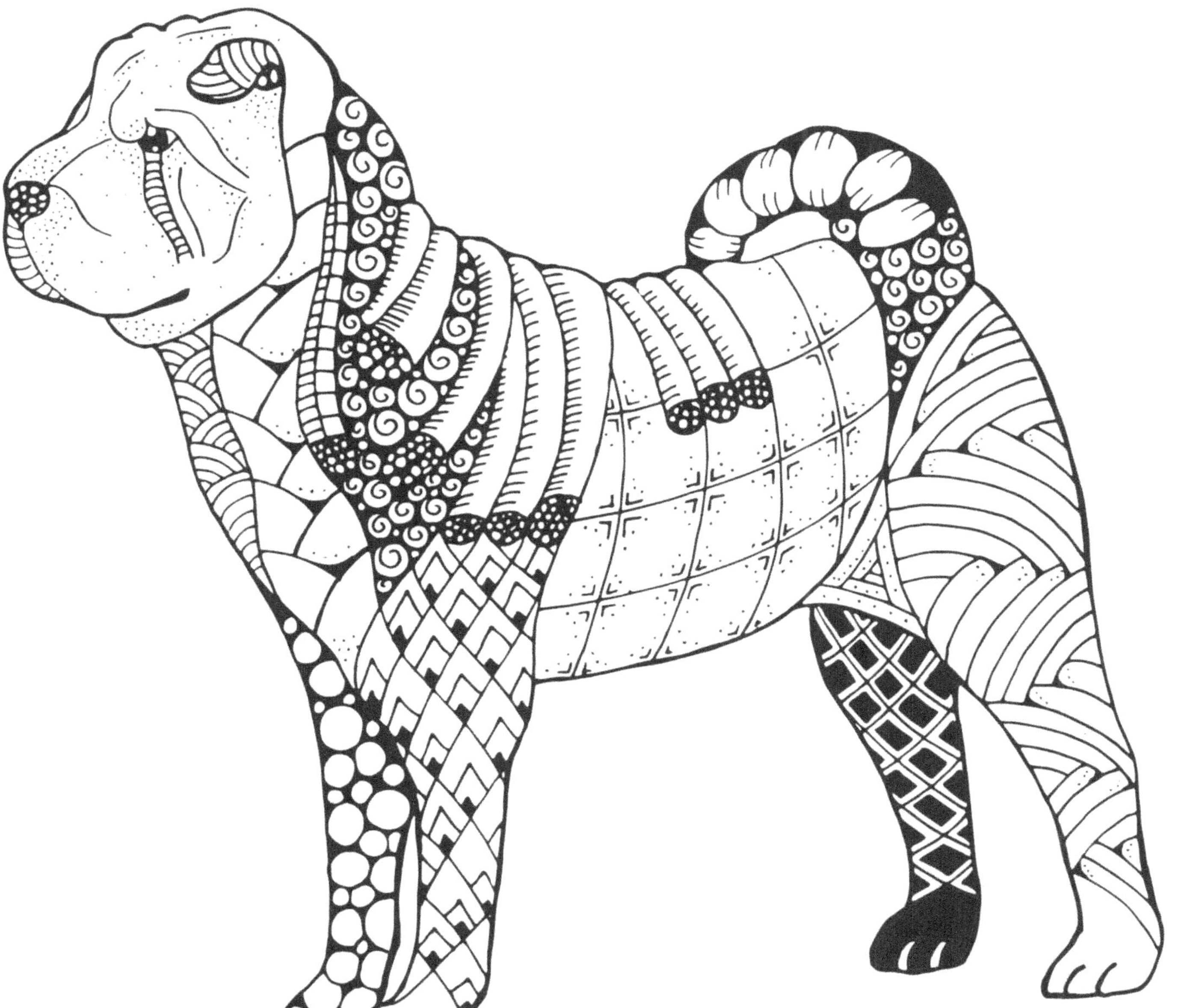

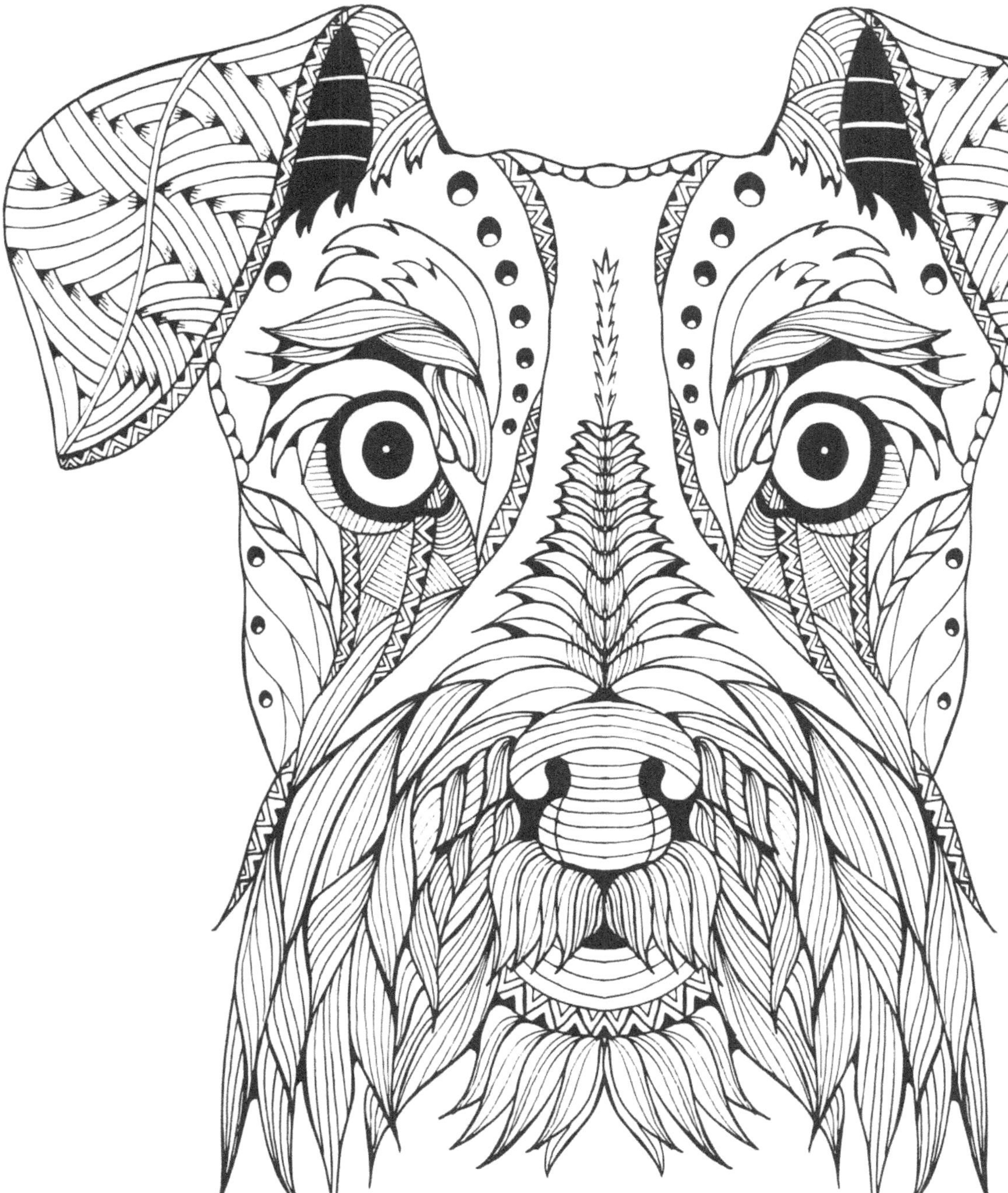

www.ingramcontent.com/pod-product-compliance
Lightning Source LLC
Chambersburg PA
CBHW081644220526
45468CB00009B/2555